THE STUFF OF SURVIVAL

A compilation of
recipes and health tips
by George Vandeman and Don Hawley

Published by

it is written

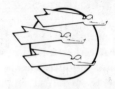

A full message telecast
presented by your friends
the Seventh-day Adventists

Box O
Thousand Oaks, CA 91360
©Copyright 1978

Printed by Center Graphics
LITHO IN USA

People do strange things sometimes. A young husband suddenly turns violent. A wife walks out on her family without warning. A teenager vowed he would never drink—but he does. A girl can't find her willpower anywhere when someone suggests drugs. A young man is likely to be committed to a mental institution if his strange behavior is ever repeated.

Family and friends are quick to blame. They don't understand. And the victims themselves are baffled. Why have they suddenly come unglued?

Could it be—is it possible—that innocent-looking menus have been tampering with the mind? There is always danger in oversimplifying a critical situation, but is it not reasonable to look carefully at the "stuff" we put into our bodies for some light on such baffling problems?

A young woman stepped into a doctor's office and was seated. She looked exhausted.

"I can hardly get any real sleep," she began. "Last night it was a little better. I only got up to iron my sheets five times."

The doctor wondered if he had heard correctly. "Did you say you got up to iron your sheets five times?"

"Yes, that's what I said."

She went on to explain. It seems that she simply couldn't stand the slightest wrinkle. If she felt one, she couldn't go to sleep. She had to get out of bed and iron her sheets. She had done this as many as twenty-five times in a single night. But last night hadn't been so bad. It was only five times!

As the doctor talked with her, he soon discovered the trouble. She was evidently a very hungry person. But she was living on nothing but bread and milk twice a day. Her food intake was the semi-starvation level.

There are other instances almost as tragic. There was the wife of a young attorney, happily married. Suddenly one night, without warning, she rushed over to the fireplace, took one of her husband's golf trophies from the mantel, and threw it through the window. She ran screaming from the house and didn't come back for three hours. The next day she asked her husband how the window got broken!

She had been on a reducing diet.

There was a young man who was suffering from severe claustrophobia—fear of small enclosures. Believe it or not, he had been unable to take a bath or a shower for over five years. He simply couldn't stay in the bathroom long enough to shower without being overcome by sheer panic!

He had been eating nothing but hamburger. Well, he said he "balanced" it with coffee and skim milk. And he smoked cigarettes incessantly.

There was the eighteen-year-old girl who described herself as a mental case. She was afraid of glass doors and big glass windows, stairways, elevators, bridges, tunnels, traffic, and germs.

Her diet was practically all refined carbohydrate foods. She recovered in a few weeks after changing her eating pattern.

These are extreme cases. I'm not suggesting that you won't be able to take a shower if you eat hamburger! Or that you will start throwing things through the window if you go on a reducing diet! Or that you will be afraid of everything from elevators to germs if your diet isn't perfectly balanced!

Nevertheless, it is common knowledge in medical and nutritional circles that *diet does influence behavior.* And because diet is so important to how we feel and how we act, let's take a closer look at one aspect of diet. Some have called it "that vegetarian thing."

There is an old story about a science professor in a boys' school. He had an uncanny knowledge of animal life. You could show him the bone of an animal, and he would name the animal. You could show him the scale of a fish, and he would not only name the fish but tell you about its habits. Animal life was his world.

One day the boys decided to play a little trick on the professor. They took the skeleton of a bear and stuffed it. Then they sewed over it the skin of a lion. On its head they fastened the horns of a Texas steer, and on its feet they glued the hoofs of a wild buffalo.

They spent a good many nights on the trick, and they did a pretty good job. Then one afternoon when the professor was taking a nap, they tiptoed into his study and set up the monstrosity. From outside the door they let out an unearthly growl such as had never been heard before.

Well, the professor woke up, the story says, tumbled off his cot, and stood bolt upright. His reaction was enough to justify all the time they had spent on the trick. But then through their peepholes they saw a surprising thing. The professor rubbed his eyes, looked at the teeth, the horns, and finally at the split hoofs. The he said, loud enough for the peepholers to hear, "Thank goodness! It's herbivorous, not carnivorous!" And went back to finish his nap.

The professor knew that any animal with horns and split hoofs is a vegetarian, and would prefer hay or grass to a sleeping professor.

Well, how do you react to a person who is a vegetarian? If you are like most people, you probably consider him harmless, even if you do think he is strangely put together—and go back to your nap.

Vegetarianism, however, is experiencing a surprising

new prosperity—largely due to the health-food movement that is sweeping the country. But people are giving up their steaks for a wide variety of other reasons too—economic, humane, psychological, and spiritual.

One of the most popular reasons—aside from the high cost of meat—is the conviction that the slaughter of animals for food is morally wrong. And then many see the vegetarian way of life as part of an attempt to escape from our mechanized society.

Hollywood, of course, has not escaped the vegetarian bandwagon. Meat seems to be "out" with a great many so-called "in " people. And if we were to do a little table-hopping among the celebrities we would hear some interesting reasons for their choice of diet.

Efrem Zimbalist, Jr., says, "I became a vegetarian . . . out of curiosity. Though I still love meat, I've remained a vegetarian simply because I feel so marvelous. . . . I have more energy and stamina."

Candice Bergen feels that the slaughter of animals is primitive and cruel. She says, "I was becoming more and more conscious of the insanity around me. Killing animals to feed us seemed to me a part of that insanity. First it seemed unappetizing and then it became disgusting. Finally, it seemed so primitive, so cruel, really horrid!" She says, "I think I became a vegetarian so I could look animals in the face."

Susan St. James has an interesting angle. She strongly believes that you can tell a vegetarian by his disposition. She says, "There's a calm that comes over you and a tremendous peace of mind when you're around vegetarians. You relate to animals a lot better, because the animals sense that you're not going to kill them and they give you faith."

As for memorable vegetarians, who is better known than the outstanding critic, George Bernard Shaw? He lived to be ninety-four. And he said, "The enormity of eating scorched, defunct animals becomes impossible the moment it becomes a conscious act, for on such a diet a man cannot do his finest work of which he is capable."

And, still in the past, there was Charles Spurgeon of London, the Billy Graham of the last century. He said, "I have lived on a purely vegetarian diet and am a one-hundred-percent better man for it, which convinces me others can do so, too."

And John Wesley, the famed pioneer of the Methodist Church. Evidently he was a vegetarian. His journals so indicate. And it is reported that he once said, "Thank God, since I gave up the eating of the flesh of animals I have bidden adieu to all the ills my flesh was heir to."

We could go on. Even Martin Luther, the rugged German reformer, wrote in a way that would lead one to believe that he was deeply impressed with the vegetarian way of life. Evidently this vegetarian thing is not new.

Some may say, "But vegetarians miss an awful lot."

Yes, they do.

One thing they miss is the risk of contracting a variety of diseases that are transmitted to humans through the handling and use of meat.

But you say, "I'm very careful about the quality of the meat I buy."

Perhaps so. But every housewife is at the mercy of the meat packer. If the packer does not exercise care, then it really doesn't matter how careful you are. You may take home only the choicest cut. But what was on the chopping block before it?

Statistics of the San Francisco Health Department on one occasion, I understand, showed that six out of every ten hog carcasses contained trichinae. Horrified, the county health officer sent inspectors with their microscopes out into the packing plants and butcher shops to find out if it was spreading to other meats. They found that, among other means of transmission, butchers' blocks were simply crawling with trichinae. Disease was being transmitted from these blocks to almost every piece of meat leaving the shops.

What about poultry? Isn't it different? Isn't it safe? Evidently here lies a danger too. An Associated Press dispatch appearing in the Seattle *Times* says, "A government panel of scientists has recommended that chickens bearing cancer virus be allowed on the market as long as the birds don't look too repugnant."

What about fish? Surely they are clean. After all, they take a bath every day. Yet a government bulletin reveals that in some mountain streams cancer is epidemic, particularly among trout, and that sometimes as many as nine out of ten have the disease.

Yes, one misses a lot by being a vegetarian.

And here's another angle. Vegetarians on the whole have a lower blood cholesterol level and have fewer heart attacks. And the *Journal of The American Medical Association* on one occasion stated that "a vegetarian diet can prevent . . . 97 percent of our coronary occlusions."

Really, have vegetarians missed anything worth having?

If you are interested, and of course it is a personal matter of decision, a person could become a vegetarian for a variety of reasons. By refusing to eat meat you could protest the violence in our civilization. You could protest the carelessness of the meat-packing industry. Or your vegetarianism could be an ecological protest. A vegetarian can be supported by one third the land required to feed a meat eater.

Yes, you could become a vegetarian out of protest. But fortunately there is an even better reason for making the change. It could be your way of responding to God's invitation to eat that which is good. Isaiah 55:2, LB reads:

8

"Why spend your money on foodstuffs that don't give you strength? Why pay for groceries that don't do you any good? Listen and I'll tell you where to get good food that fattens up the soul."

That's interesting. Foodstuffs that don't give you strength. But most people think that meat gives you strength—that meat is your source of energy. Is that true? Dr. Stare of Harvard University doesn't think so. He says,

"Lumberjacks may demand plenty of red meat, but that demand rests on habit and not on nutritional or medical basis."

MAN'S FIRST DIET

Back at the beginning of man's creation God started man out with a new body. And He told him what to put into it.

"And look! I have given you the seed-bearing plants throughout the earth, and all the fruit trees for your food." Genesis 1:29,LB.

A new body. And how to feed it. What to put into it to keep it operating at peak efficiency. A sort of owner's manual, you see.

I will never forget the first new car that I ever owned. The dealer brought it out, all bright and shining. He left the motor running, and turned on the radio, and stepped out. He held the door open and told me to take over.

I drove it out so very carefully. I went only a block or so and pulled over to the curb. Then I reached into the glove compartment and took out the owner's manual. I wanted to see just what to put into my new car. I wanted to do just what the manufacturer told me. No car ever had better care than that car did. I followed the manufacturer's instructions.

Why don't we do that with our bodies? God made our

bodies—and gave us an owner's manual. He told us how to keep them running at top efficiency. Why don't we follow the Creator's instructions? Why don't we take care of our bodies as carefully as we do our cars?

In the beginning, of course, everybody ate natural foods. And those foods kept a man going a long time. Adam lived 950 years. Methuselah lived 969. Many of those men lived three, four, six, seven hundred years.

Then came the Flood of Noah's day. And after the Flood, because the natural foods had all been destroyed, God gave man permission, as an emergency measure, to eat the flesh of animals. Not all animals, you understand—only certain ones that God designated as fit for food.

Now God knew perfectly well that the use of flesh food, permitted as an emergency measure, would be continued. He may have had still another reason for permitting it. Men before the Flood lived very long lives, and bent on evil as they were, they could do a lot of damage and cause a lot of ruin with a lifespan like that. Imagine a few Hitlers loose in the world—and living seven or eight hundred years!

God saw that it was best to shorten man's lifespan. And He knew that the use of flesh food would accomplish it. Take a look sometime in your Bible, and notice the tremendous drop in man's lifespan immediately after the Flood.

But now we come down to the time of Jesus. Jesus, we are told, ate fish. Fish that have fins and scales were designated by God as clean. Fish formed a large part of the diet of the people of His day.

There are those who say that since the distinction between clean and unclean meats was a part of the Law of Moses, which is no longer in effect, we should disregard that instruction today. We should keep in mind, however, that it was God who said the animals were unclean. Would a law going out of effect change the animals? Would an animal that was unclean the day before Jesus died be clean the day after He died? If you are interested in a detailed list of those permitted and those not permitted, you will find it in Leviticus 11 and Deuteronomy 14.

The pig, for instance, is one of the animals God calls unclean and not fit for food. The hog is a scavenger.

Someone may be reasoning, "Why did God create scavengers and animals that were not fit for food?"

In the first place, according to Scripture, animals were never intended for food.

But there was another restriction that God made when He permitted the use of flesh food after the Flood. The blood was not to be eaten. It was to be drained from the meat. And did you ever eat a steak from which all the blood had been drained? I assure you that you'd never want another. It is the blood that gives meat its flavor. And that blood is carrying the waste products of the animal. Not a happy thought, is it?

It is interesting, and significant, that John the Baptist, whose special work was to prepare the way for the ministry of Jesus, was instructed to eat a completely vegetarian diet. The "locusts" he ate were pods from a tree—not insects.

And John was a type, a representative of the people who give God's last message to the world, to prepare the way for Christ's second coming. Is it possible that God might ask something special of us in view of the critical days ahead?

If you are thinking of feeding the starving people of the world, meat is not the answer. It's too expensive to produce. An acre of cereal crops will provide five times more protein than if the same acre were used for meat production. And that land will yield ten times more protein if you plant beans or some other legume on that acre. As a food machine the cow is just hopelessly inefficient!

Is it possible that flesh food is not only unnecessary for survival but that it actually works against survival? Check it out by futher study and observation and see where it leads you. The results can be most satisfactory.

There are difficult days ahead. We will need all the strength we can get—not only physical but moral. There will be vastly important decisions to make. Can we afford to be impairing the mind in any way whatever at a time like this?

The long and costly experiment with sin is almost over. God's original plan will soon be restored. And in God's country there will be no death, no violence, nothing to mar the happiness of God's redeemed people. There will be lions there. And there will be lambs. And the Bible says they will lie down together. But what will the lions eat? It says they will eat straw. And again I ask, Could there be a connection between diet and disposition?

Unquestionably death is our enemy. One day death will be destroyed. But why hold on to it now—in any form?

This booklet does not suggest a rash move. It does not suggest cleaning out the refrigerator immediately and changing your life-style without preparing thoughtfully. Rather it invites you to make an intelligent, carefully planned experiment with change.

And now to a question many have been asking. Is vegetarianism a matter of health, or a matter of morals? The apostle Paul says,

"Whether you eat or drink, or whatever you are doing, do all for the honor of God." I Corinthians 10:31, NEB.

Whatever you do, do for His honor. Yes. But why are eating and drinking involved? Again the apostle Paul has the answer:

"Do you not know that your body is a shrine of the indwelling Holy Spirit, and the Spirit is God's gift to you? You do not belong to yourselves; you were bought at a

12

price. Then honour God in your body." I Corinthians 6:19,20, NEB.

Loma Linda University is beginning a study that will last five years. They will be studying people. They will be studying Seventh-day Adventists.

Why Seventh-day Adventists? Because for some reason Adventists have only about half as much cancer as the general population. And the government has given the university a grant of $800,000 to find out why.

You may be aware that Seventh-day Adventists do not smoke or drink. The fact that they do not smoke would explain their very low incidence of lung cancer. But there are other kinds of cancer too. Why the low incidence of these also?

There must be something about the Adventist life-style that is responsible for these impressive statistics. Scientists suspect it may be their dietary habits. Because Adventists are largely vegetarians.

Well, it will be interesting to watch the study as it progresses. Is it possible that meat, the very food Americans consider most indispensable—and a shortage of which is considered a national emergency—is it possible that our meat diet could have something to do with our staggering cancer statistics? It's something to think about.

Do you long for the day when all of us, if we choose, cured of our rebellion, can be restored to radiant health? Jesus, when He was here, was so impatient for that day that He walked through villages and healed all their sick.

He fed five thousand one day with miracle bread. He was evidently looking forward to the day when He could offer them fruit from the tree of life—instead of bread. He can hardly wait for that day!

On the very last page of the Bible it says, "Blessed are they that do His commandments, that they may have right to the tree of life, and may enter in through the gates into the city." (Revelation 22:14)

Who will have access to the tree? Who will eat its invigorating fruit and never die? Those who have kept God's commandments. Not only His moral law. But His laws of health. Those who have taken care of their bodies. Those who have made right decisions—because their minds have been kept clear enough to make them!

Here are helpful hints found in a handy little book titled *Commonsense Nutrition*. One chapter suggests several hints for meal planning:

1. Have a set time for planning menus, if possible, and think of each day as a unit rather than each meal separately.

2. Plan menus in advance. Try a weekly or several-days-in-advance menu with an accompanying market list. This saves money and time by making marketing and meal preparation more efficient. The menu plan should be flexible enough to allow you to take advantage of good buys, use leftovers, and provide for unforeseen circumstances.

3. Stay within your budget. The lower the allowance, the greater the challenge! You can save money by using foods in season, canning, drying, or freezing when seasonal foods are plentiful and by doubling or tripling some recipes and freezing the extra for later use.

4. Use the daily food guide (or four food groups) as the basis of menu planning. Adapt the guide to each member of your family, from the toddler to grandparents. Include dishes the whole family enjoys. Your personal preferences should not dominate the menu planning; neither should food be avoided that one dislikes.

5. To avoid monotony, change the pattern of a meal now and then. Plan it around the salad or soup or

have a one-dish meal plus an interesting dessert.

6. Serve a wide selection of food from meal to meal, vary your methods of preparation, and include foods of different texture at each meal. A rule sometimes suggested is to include at each meal something soft, something crisp and chewy and something firm.

7. Serve heaviest meals in the morning and at noon if practical. Studies of both school children and adults of all ages show that greater mental and physical energy result all day if a fourth to a third of the daily nutrients are included at breakfast. (Cary, Vyhmeister, Hudson, *Commonsense Nutrition,* pp. 25-26)

If you follow these suggestions, you will find that it becomes increasingly easy to maintain a vegetarian diet.

The most important thing to remember when making the transition to a vegetarian diet is to do it gradually. Heavy meat eaters should not suddenly stop eating flesh food, but slowly eliminate it from the diet over a period of time.

You should also remember that as you eliminate flesh food, you should replace it in your diet with adequate plant proteins. If you are careful about these two items, you should not have any difficulty changing your life-style to that of a vegetarian.

It is most important that your new vegetarian dishes are appetizing ones. One of the purposes of the recipe section of this booklet is to help you with just that.

Many of the recipes you'll find on the following pages are among the most unusual you will ever taste. Just look through the recipe section and discover how tantalizing a vegetarian entree can be.

RECIPES

We know you want to enjoy food that is not only delicious, but also nutritious. Here are a few suggestions that may be helpful as they are applied to any of the recipes you use.

EGGS

It is best not to use too many eggs, even in cooking. If a recipe calls for no more than from one-fourth to one-third egg per serving, there is no problem. Beyond this, one might want to substitute Fleischman's Eggbeaters, Second Nature products or Worthington Scramblers, refrigerated egg products with most of the cholesterol-laden yolks removed.

Or you may desire to do the substituting yourself. If a recipe calls for four eggs, try using two complete eggs plus four egg whites. If six eggs are indicated, use three eggs along with four egg whites. If six eggs are indicated, use three eggs along with four egg whites. It isn't likely you will notice any actual difference in the dish you are preparing, and you'll be healthier for the substitution.

CHEESE

Cheese is another popular item in the American diet that causes some concern. It is best to use a minimal amount, and then to substitute the low-fat, low cholesterol cheeses now available on the market.

Cheese on the recommended list include: cottage cheese, Neufchatel, cream cheese, ricotta, yogurt, hoop cheese, and Baker's cheese. Others that are not too objectionable: Milano, Monterey Jack, and Longhorn.

MEAT ANALOGS

Some of the following recipes call for meat analogs, commercially prepared meat substitutes available in an increasing number of markets and health food stores.

While not essential for a well-balanced vegetarian diet, they are a favorite of many vegetarians for their taste and texture. People in the process of changing over to a vegetarian diet appreciate them for the meat-like qualities they add to the diet.

You will find that in many of your own recipes calling for ground beef, the use of vegetarian burger products will produce a dish which is just as flavorful and much more nutritious.

Complete lines of these canned, frozen and dehydrated foods are available throughout the country. The two companies in America producing the largest volume of these meat analogs are: Loma Linda Foods, 11503 Pierce Street, Riverside, CA 92505, and Worthington Foods, Worthington, OH 43085. Contact these companies for more information on meat analogs as well as for help in locating nearby retail outlets for these products.

And now, try some of these tasty recipes in your own kitchen . . .

HOMESTYLE BEAN SOUP

1	pound package navy beans, dry
1	bay leaf
2	teaspoons salt
1	cup onion, chopped
1	cup celery, chopped
2	teaspoons seasoned salt
2	envelopes G. Washington Broth or 1 tablespoon chicken-like seasoning
1	cup carrots, grated or chopped
1/3	cup parsley flakes
2	tablespoons margarine

Soak beans overnight. Pour off water and add enough water to cover the beans two inches above the beans (two quarts or more). Bring to a boil and then simmer. Add bay leaf and salt. Let simmer one hour before adding onions, celery and rest of seasonings. Let simmer another hour and add the carrots the last 15 minutes, as well as parsley flakes. Add the margarine and more seasonings, if needed.

Nellie Vandeman
(Wife of George E. Vandeman,
It Is Written Director-Speaker)

SPLIT PEA SOUP

1/2 pound green split peas, dry
2   quarts water
1/4 teaspoon Accent
1/2 teaspoon paprika
1/8 teaspoon celery salt
1/2 teaspoon onion powder
1/2 teaspoon olive oil
1/2 bay leaf
2   teaspoons savory seasoning
1   teaspoon parsley flakes

Cook peas in water until soft. Place in blender and blend until smooth. Add the Accent, paprika, celery salt, onion powder, olive oil, bay leaf and savory. Place in top of double boiler and cook for 15 minutes. Add parsley to soup and cook for additional 30 minutes.

LENTIL SOUP

1½ cups lentils, dry
7   cups water
salt and season to taste

Cook 20 minutes.

Add:
1   medium potato, diced
1   medium onion, diced
2   small carrots, diced
3   tablespoons margarine
2   fresh tomatoes, chopped

Cook until lentils are soft and vegetables done. 50—60 minutes. Sprinkle with Parmesan cheese (optional).

VEGETABLE SOUP
(Borscht)

2   cups grated beets
1   quart water
1/2 cup beet greens
1/2 cup string beans, cut up
1/2 cup carrots, diced
1/4 cup parsnips, diced
1/2 cup cabbage, shredded
1/2 cup green peas
1   cup potatoes, diced
salt to taste
1   quart tomato juice
1   tablespoon parsley
1/2 teaspoon dill weed
1/4 cup onion, chopped fine
1   cup sweet cream

Cook fresh beets and remove skins, grate. Prepare the rest of the vegetables as directed. Place all vegetables in a large kettle and cook until almost done. Add tomato juice and seasoning and simmer a few minutes. Sauté onion in 1 teaspoon margarine until brown. Add sweet cream and simmer a few minutes. Add cream and onions to hot soup and immediately set burner on low. (If it boils, it sometimes curdles.)

More water or juice may be added if the soup is too thick.

Good if made in advance, but do not add the cream until you reheat it and always heat the cream before adding.

MELON WITH LENTIL SALAD

1	cup lentils, dry
3	cups water
1	teaspoon salt
2	tablespoons oil
1/3	cup lemon juice, fresh
1/4	teaspoon garlic, minced
2	teaspoons dry mint leaves, crushed
1	tablespoon parsley, chopped
1	onion, thinly sliced or
	2-3 green onions, chopped
3	small fragrant ripe melons

Cook lentils in water and simmer about 30 minutes or until lentils are tender but not mushy. Add salt and keep covered for ten minutes more off heat. Mix oil, lemon, garlic, mint, parsley and onions. Toss with lentils gently. Cover and refrigerate one hour or longer to blend flavors. To serve, cut melons in half crosswise and use as container for the lentil salad to be eaten with spoon. Serves six.

RICE AND CHICKEN SALAD

1½   cups chicken-style soyameat, diced
1½   cups rice, cooked
1½   cups celery, chopped
1/4   cup onion, diced
1/2   cup green pepper, chopped
1   tablespoon lemon juice
3/4   cup mayonnaise

Mix together all ingredients except mayonnaise. Cover and chill three to four hours or overnight. Add mayonnaise. Arrange on lettuce leaves in a salad bowl. Garnish with parsley or in petal tomato cup.

Nellie Vandeman

SOYBEAN SALAD

2   cups soybeans, cooked
1   cup celery and leaves, finely chopped
1/4   cup onions, finely chopped
1/3   cup salad dressing
       watercress

Mix all ingredients but watercress and let it marinate 3-4 hours in refrigerator. Garnish with water cress just before serving.

CARROT RING WITH GREEN PEA FILLING

Carrot Ring:

2   cups brown rice, cooked
2   cups low-fat cottage cheese
2   cups carrots, grated
1   large onion, chopped
1   tablespoon chicken-like seasoning
2   tablespoons parsley, chopped
1/2 teaspoon thyme
4   egg whites

Mix all ingredients. Pack into oiled ring mold. Bake at 350° for 45-55 minutes. Let stand 2-3 minutes before unmolding. Fill center with green vegetable. Serves 6-8.

Green Pea Filling:

1   cup mushrooms, sliced (fresh or canned)
1   package green peas, frozen
1   teaspoon beef-style seasoning
1   cup liquid
2   tablespoons cornstarch or arrowroot

Drain mushroom liquid and add water to make one cup. Simmer mushrooms, peas, seasoning in 1/2 cup liquid and stir into vegetables. Continue stirring over medium heat until sauce thickens. Pour vegetables in center of carrot ring and serve.

FETTUCINI AND SPINACH CASSEROLE

2   recipes whole wheat noodles
2   tablespoons olive oil
2   cloves garlic, minced or
    1/4 teaspoon dry minced garlic
2   packages (10 ounces) frozen spinach, chopped,
    thawed and drained
1   teaspoon salt
1   teaspoon basil
1/2 cup fresh parsley, chopped or
    1/4 cup dry parsley
2   cups (1 pound) part skim ricotta or
    low fat cottage cheese
1   cup skim milk

Cook noodles in salted water until firm tender or 'al dente'; drain. Meanwhile, in hot oil in skillet sauté garlic and spinach stirring about two minutes. Add salt, basil and parsley and cover. Turn heat to low and let cook another minute or two. Blend cheese and milk thoroughly and stir lightly into spinach mixture another couple of minutes. Toss spinach cheese mixture with noodles. Turn out on a heated serving dish and garnish with pimento strips. If you prefer you may sprinkle with grated Parmesan cheese. Serves 8-10.

Select any three

of these outstanding books by George Vandeman for only two dollars

This offer makes it possible for you to receive three of George Vandeman's books for the special price of only two dollars. Read the description of each book carefully. Then *check your choices* on the enclosed envelope, *enclose two dollars*, and drop it in the mail. All books are approximately ninety-six pages. The three you choose will be mailed promptly postpaid. You may select as many groups of three as you desire and in any combination.

If the reply envelope is missing, send your request to the address below. Be sure your three choices are clearly indicated, that your name and address are carefully printed, and that two dollars is enclosed. Write to:

In the United States:
IT IS WRITTEN
Box 0
Thousand Oaks, CA 91360

In Canada:
IT IS WRITTEN
Box 1010
Oshawa, Ontario

In Australia:
IT IS WRITTEN
148 Fox Valley Rd.
Wahroonga, N.S.W.

Prices subject to change.

How to Live With a Tiger

Have you ever felt as if you have a tiger inside—and you don't know how to tame him? Then you'll want to ask for

How to Live With a Tiger

This book is the story of George Vandeman's personal encounter with the claims of the Lord Jesus Christ, and of the night he shook his fist at God—and what happened then. It also shares the priceless secrets of Christian living that he discovered—and that you can too in the pages of this book. Whatever your feelings of frustration or defeat, you will find help here.

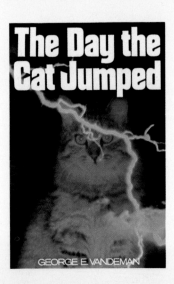

The Day the Cat Jumped

GEORGE E. VANDEMAN

If you care about the future, if you care about your own destiny and that of your loved ones, be sure to ask for

The Day the Cat Jumped

This is a book about how not to be surprised by the return of Christ to this earth. About how to identify the real Christ and how to spot an impostor. About the secret rapture —as the Scriptures really tell it. About the sequence of events that happen *after* the second coming of Christ. About Israel and Armageddon.

If you want to be sure you don't kneel down before a masquerading impostor, thinking him to be Christ —this book is a *must!*

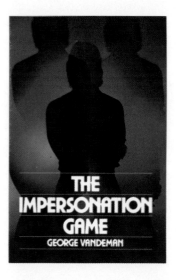

Unless you want to be the victim of a worldwide hoax, you desperately need the information in

The Impersonation Game

This book will make you aware of a massive deception that is sweeping the world. It will tell you who the impersonators are, what they are up to, what their goals are, and how to recognize their propaganda. Not to be informed could be fatal!

Are you more aware than ever that you have only one life to live— only one body, only one heart, only one mind? Then you'll want to select

How to Burn Your Candle

You'll read about the new medicine, about the ultimate miracle drug that we'll never find, about how to deal with stress, and how to stop smoking. You'll discover the relationship between our eating and our behavior. If you're wondering if the vegetarian way of life is for you, this book will help you decide. You'll find a chapter on healing, one about the winds of the witches, and one about the angel in the slot machine. Sound intriguing? Then select this book!

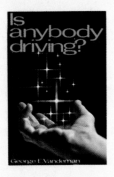

If the six o'clock news makes you wonder if we're riding a runaway planet completely out of control, you will want to read

Is Anybody Driving?

This is a book about how to live without all the answers. How to be certain in an uncertain world. How to face the future unafraid. What to do about loneliness and despair. You'll discover that it helps to know who's driving—and where you're going and why. It's a book that will take the bugs out of your faith. And chances are you'll decide with the author that things aren't really so bad. Try it!

If you are young—or young at heart—and you want to be free—but you wonder if anybody really is—your choice will be

Sail Your Own Seas

Is there such a thing as free choice? Or is it only an illusion? If you are the independent type, or if you have a touch of the rebel in you, you'll like this unusual book about the dangerous—and sometimes tricky—business of being on your own. About Cadillacs and nine-year-olds and irrevocable driver's licenses. About wrong-way streets and fences and automatic nightmares. A book that's different!

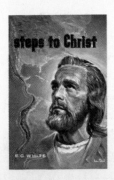

If you feel an emptiness in your life and know that Christ is the answer, but you don't know just how to go about accepting Him—then ask for

Steps to Christ

This book, unlike the others, is not by George Vandeman, but by his favorite author—Ellen White. It's a book that is priceless and timeless. Sixteen million copies have been printed to date. It has been translated into a hundred languages. In simple, understandable words it talks about the love of God, how God feels about us, about repentance and confession and forgiveness—how to come to Christ and be rid of guilt.

If you have ever wished you could push aside the strange, impenetrable curtain that makes death a mystery, then select

Destination Life

Have you wondered long hours about what happens after death? Have you been both fascinated and frightened by the claims of spiritism? Have you been perplexed by the exploits of hypnotism, the almost incredible accounts of psychic phenomena? Have you watched with captive interest the predictions of the crystal ball? This book is for you.

If you have tried to stop smoking—and discovered it isn't easy—your first choice may be

Papa, Are You Going to Die?

This is not a book about death. It is not a book about what happens to a man when he dies. Rather, it is intended to help you deal with stress in this pell-mell generation, to help you avoid the fatigue you were never meant to have, to help you protect your heart from cardiac accident. It is intended to help you postpone the day when the rope breaks. And in the meantime, life can be more meaningful and more fun!

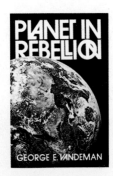

If you are interested in life on other worlds— battles in outer space—and mysteries in our skies, then ask for

Planet in Rebellion

Is there life on other worlds? Are we being watched? Are our stellar neighbors trying to contact us? In this cosmic drama are we only the spectators? Or are we ourselves the actors— playing in the final act—and without a rehearsal?

This book is approaching a million copies. And there's one for you.

Hammers in the Fire

George E. Vandeman

If you are a doubter, and you would like to believe—at least you are willing to consider the evidence—then the book for you is

Hammers in the Fire

This unusual book is the story of hammers. Hammers in the fire of a long and still unfinished controversy. It is also the story of a Book that through the centuries, quietly but persistently, has been wearing the hammers out one by one. Wearing them out with the help of spades and rocks and water, honeybees and stars. And fuzzy wuzzy angels.

If you are interested in getting married, or staying married, you will want to select

Happiness Wall to Wall

Here are some realistic formulas for marriage that lasts. What to do when the raft comes apart. What to do when husbands won't talk. What to do when wives forget to be attractive. What to do when infidelity suddenly appears in your home.

This is a book for the married and those about to be married. Others will like it too.

If you are interested in God's reaction to accounts of creation by men who weren't there be sure to ask for

A Day to Remember

The author grapples with prime issues, basic foundations, challenging revelations. But he does it kindly. He touches controversy without dogmatism, yet with no hint of compromise.

The book begins with the story of an atomic accident, offers a surprising account of a day hijacked in the Dark Ages, and warns of an approaching collision of loyalties when bigotry will return and no man can buy or sell unless—

If you are tired of uncertainty, if you would like to know some things for sure, you will want to choose

Tying Down the Sun

Does it trouble you that scientists keep changing their minds about our beginnings? In this book you will find a thrilling array of evidence—all of it exciting and much of it new—that will topple your uncertainty once for all. Surprising evidence will happily convince you that when God said He created the earth He really did, and that when He said it was good it really was!

If you are interested in the vegetarian way of life and would like some helpful recipes, you will want

The Stuff of Survival

a book that explains how to make such an involved change in life style. Mrs. Vandeman's favorites are included.

(Revised and enlarged 1978)

Bible Study?

Of course—

Join the growing number of people who are turning to Bible study for answers to important questions.

If you have enjoyed the "It Is Written" telecast you will certainly appreciate the "It Is Written" Bible Study plan. Simply print the words "Bible Study" with your name and address on a separate piece of paper and send it to

"It Is Written"
Box 0, Thousand Oaks, California 91360.

Special Offer

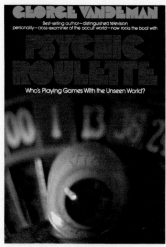

Psychic Roulette

George Vandeman's latest book on the startling world of the occult!

We are playing games with partners we cannot see . . . and we would be shocked if we knew their identity!

Just a few of the intriguing chapter titles: Typewriter in a Trance . . . The Script in the Crystal Ball . . . How to Tell a Fake . . .

Paper, $3.00.

Vegetarianism Why be a Vegetarian?

If you would like to beat the high cost of meat—and eat more healthfully at the same time—you will want this book.

It gives you reliable up-to-date facts about vegetarianism and its advantages. Also you will find here suggested menus and recipes for delicious vegetarian dishes. If you would like to eat better—and save money at the same time—this is a must.

Paper, $1.50.

These books are not a part of the three-for-two-dollar offer—but for your convenience you may order from the IT IS WRITTEN office at Box 0, Thousand Oaks, CA 91360.

WHOLE WHEAT NOODLES

Stir together:

1/2 cup whole wheat flour
1/2 cup all purpose flour
1/2 teaspoon salt
1/4 teaspoon onion powder (optional)

Beat together:

1/3 cup water
2   tablespoons oil
1   teaspoon lecithin (optional)

Add liquid to dry ingredients slowly, moistening evenly. Knead lightly a few times. Cover and let rest about 10 minutes. On lightly floured surface, roll dough very thin. Let stand 20 minutes. Roll up loosely and cut in strips. Spread out and let dry two hours or more. Store in container, or cook immediately in large amount of boiling salted water for 8-12 minutes or until firm tender. Makes about 2½ cups cooked noodles.

STUFFED ZUCCHINI

2/3   cup textured vegetable protein (TVP)*
Juice of 1/2 lemon
1   tablespoon oil
1   tablespoon parsley flakes
      dash of minced garlic
1/2   teaspoon salt
1/2   onion, chopped
1   cup brown rice, cooked
(you may use 1/2 cup uncooked white rice if you prefer)
3   zucchini squash or summer squash
2   cups tomato juice

Soak the TVP in equal amount of water as directed for
five or more minutes along with lemon juice, oil, parsley,
garlic, and salt. Stir in the onion and rice into TVP
mixture. Cut zucchini in half lengthwise and scoop out
seeds. Salt cavity lightly and stuff with TVP filling. Place
in pan and pour tomato juice carefully around zucchini.
Simmer or bake covered for 45 minutes or until done.
Note: This filling is good for cabbage rolls, green peppers, eggplant, and stuffed tomatoes or onions.

*1 cup garbanzos, cooked or canned, or 1/2 cup
  chopped nuts can be substituted for the TVP.

PROSAGE PATE

1	pound Prosage*
1	clove garlic, minced fine
3	ounces low fat cream cheese
1/2	teaspoon basil
1	tablespoon parsley
1/3	cup Stripple Zips*, crushed
2	tablespoons mayonnaise

Mix all ingredients except Stripple Zips together until well blended. Add Stripple Zips. Mix to distribute evenly. Chill. Serve with crackers or melba toast as an appetizer spread or as a sandwich filling.

Frosted Pate: Prepare prosage pate. Form into half a ball shape on large platter. Chill until stiff. Spread with the following "Frosting" and decorate with olives, etc.

Frosting:

8	ounces cream cheese
1	teaspoon mayonnaise
1/4	teaspoon garlic powder

*Worthington Foods products. Prosage is a sausage-type frozen meat analog. Stripple Zips are bacon-like bits and are sold in a can.

ENGLISH MUFFIN TOPPING

3/4 pound mild Longhorn cheese, grated
1 bunch green onions (white part),
    sliced or chopped
1 cup stuffed olives, chopped
1 4-ounce can ripe olives, chopped
1 4-ounce can green chiles, diced
1/4 teaspoon oregano
1/8 teaspoon garlic powder
1 4-ounce can tomato sauce

Mix well. Spread on lightly toasted English muffins. Put under broiler until bubbly before serving. (You may use hamburger buns instead of English muffins.)

Nellie Vandeman

FAT-FREE GRAVY

3½ cups vegetable broth
1/4 cup cornstarch
1 tablespoon chicken or beef-like seasoning
1 teaspoon Kitchen Bouquet
1 teaspoon onion powder

Dissolve cornstarch in 1/2 cup broth. Heat remaining broth with seasoning, Kitchen Bouquet, and onion powder. Gradually stir in cornstarch mixture. Stir constantly over medium heat until smooth and thick. May add onions, mushrooms or parsley to taste.

MUSHROOM GRAVY BEEF STYLE

1¾ cups water
2¾ teaspoons soup base beef-like flavor
2 tablespoons flour
1½ tablespoons shortening
1/2 teaspoon Kitchen Bouquet or soy sauce
1 ounce mushroom stems and pieces

Heat water in small pan and dissolve in it beef flavored soup base. In skillet, mix flour and shortening and heat. Stir in hot stock gradually until thickened. Mix in Kitchen Bouquet and the mushrooms.

EASY CHEESE SOUFFLE

1 cup milk, scalded
1 cup bread, broken in pieces
1 cup mild Longhorn cheese, grated
2 teaspoons margarine
3 eggs, separated
1/2 teaspoon salt

Put bread, cheese, margarine, and salt in bowl together. Pour hot scalded milk over this and let stand until cool. Beat egg yolks and add to mixture. Beat egg whites until stiff and fold into mixture. Pour into greased 1½ quart baking dish and bake for 20 minutes at 400°. Serve with mushroom sauce, if desired. Serves 4-6. (Knife will come out clean when finished baking.)

Nellie Vandeman

CABBAGE ROLLS

1	medium cabbage
1	cup rice, cooked
1	cup vegetarian burger
1/2	cup celery, chopped
1/2	cup onion, minced
2	tablespoons oil
1	teaspoon salt
1	tablespoon parsley, chopped
1/4	teaspoon sage
1	can tomato soup
2	tablespoons margarine

Cut around the core of the cabbage and steam for a few minutes by setting core side in water, remove leaves and save.

Sauté onion and celery in oil, add seasoning and combine with rice and vegetarian burger. Put a tablespoon of filling on a cabbage leaf and roll. Place in baking dish and cover with tomato soup and dot with margarine. Place odds and ends of cabbage leaves on top, cover and bake in 350° oven for one hour. Serve hot on a platter with sautéed onions on top.

SOY SOUFFLE

1	cup soy beans
2	cups water
1/4	cup onion, chopped
1	tablespoon Savorex*
1/2	tablespoon Smokene
1	tablespoon brewer's yeast
1/4	teaspoon salt
1	tablespoon soy sauce

Soak, until swelled, 1 cup soy beans in 2 cups water. Blend in blender until smooth. More water may be added to ease with blending. Mix with other ingredients. Pour into 9 x 13 baking dish. Bake 350° for 45-50 minutes. May be served hot as entrée. May also be served cold as sandwich filling. Can be mashed and mixed with salad dressing for excellent sandwich spread.

*A flavoring. Can substitute 2 teaspoons soy sauce plus 2 teaspoons brewer's yeast.

CHICKEN-STYLE TETRAZZINI

1¾ cups milk, skim
3   ounces mushrooms, stems and pieces
3   tablespoons green peppers, chopped
1/4 cup margarine
1/4 cup flour
2   tablespoons pimentos, chopped
1   tablespoon chicken-like flavored seasoning
6   ounces spaghetti, long
2   cups chicken-style, diced
1/3 cup Parmesan cheese

Heat milk. Cook mushrooms and peppers in margarine until tender. Mix in flour and chicken seasoning. Add hot milk. Cook and stir until thick. Add pimento and chicken-like flavoring. Mix well. While sauce is cooking, cook spaghetti until tender. Add chicken-style mixture to cooked spaghetti and mix well. Pour into ungreased 2-quart baking dish. Sprinkle with cheese. Bake in hot oven (425°) for 15 minutes or until brown.

SPINACH LOAF

2   packages frozen spinach, chopped
     (or 1 pound fresh spinach, cooked)
1/2 cup green onions, chopped
1/4 cup fresh parsley, chopped
1/4 teaspoon garlic, minced
1/4 teaspoon oregano
1   teaspoon salt
1   cup mild cheese (such as Muenster), grated
     tossed with 1 tablespoon flour
2   beaten eggs
1   5⅓ ounce can evaporated milk

Mix all ingredients and pour into buttered loaf pan. Bake 45 minutes at 350°. Run knife around edges and unmold. Garnish with broiled tomato halves if desired.

COTTAGE CHEESE-PECAN ROAST

2   eggs and 4 egg whites, beaten
2   cups Special K breakfast cereal
1½ cups cottage cheese, small curd
1/2 cup pecans, chopped
1/3 cup onions, chopped
2   tablespoons margarine, melted
2   envelopes G. Washington golden broth
     dissolved in 3 tablespoons hot water

Mix all ingredients and pour in greased 9 x 9 or 7 x 12 baking dish. Bake at 325° for 45 minutes or until knife comes out clean. Serves 8-10.

Nellie Vandeman

STIR-FRIED TOFU AND VEGETABLES

2   tablespoons oil
1   onion, thinly sliced
6   mushrooms, sliced
2   green peppers, cut in strips
1   carrot, cut in strips
1   cup bean sprouts
1   brick tofu (16-24 ounce), cut in strips
1   teaspoon chicken-like seasoning
1   tablespoon brown sugar
1/2   teaspoon ginger root, grated (optional)
2   tablespoons soy sauce
1   tablespoon cornstarch or arrowroot
1/2   cup water

Slice vegetables and tofu. Sauté in skillet or wok with barely enough oil to coat skillet. Stir lightly over high heat for 30-60 seconds. Reduce heat to low, cover and simmer about five minutes at most. In small cup mix seasonings, starch and water. Stir into vegetables mixing constantly until vegetables are coated and sauce thickens. Vegetables should be crisp tender. If they need further cooking, cover and simmer until desired doneness. For extra tang add 1 tablespoon lemon juice. Serves 4-6.

VEGETARIAN HAMBURGERS

1	19-ounce can vegetarian burger
3	eggs and 4 egg whites, beaten
1	large onion, chopped
1	green pepper, chopped
1	teaspoon sage
1	tablespoon soy sauce
1/2	cup toasted bread crumbs or Pepperidge Farm dressing
1/2	teaspoon garlic salt

Mix vegetarian burger and beaten eggs. Sauté onions and green peppers and add to burger mix. Add sage, soy sauce, bread crumbs and garlic salt. Mix well. Fry in patties. (1/2 cup mix per patty for hamburger bun).

A quick variation when in a hurry is to use 1 envelope of Lipton's Onion Soup mix instead of the onions and green pepper.

Nellie Vandeman

MUSHROOMS FLORENTINE

12 large mushrooms
2   tablespoons margarine
1   onion, chopped
1   clove garlic, pressed
1   package frozen spinach, thawed
1   egg yolk
1/2 teaspoon salt
1/8 teaspoon nutmeg
4   tablespoons Parmesan cheese

Clean mushrooms and remove stems. Melt margarine in frying pan over medium heat. Turn mushroom caps in butter and arrange cut side up in baking dish.

Dice stems. Add onion, garlic and sauté until onion is limp. Squeeze spinach DRY and add to onion. Remove from heat. Add egg, salt, nutmeg and 2 1/2 tablespoons cheese. Mound mixture into mushroom caps and sprinkle with remaining cheese. Bake at 325° for 15 minutes.

OATBURGERS

1	onion, chopped
2	tablespoons oil
2	eggs
2	tablespoons milk, canned
2	teaspoons soy sauce
2	cups oatmeal, uncooked
1	teaspoon salt
1/2	cup water
3	tablespoons soy sauce

Sauté onions in oil only until clear, not brown. Pour in mixing bowl. Add eggs, milk, soy sauce, oats, and salt. Stir well. If quick cook oats are used, set mixture aside for 10 minutes. If old-fashioned oats are used, let stand 30 minutes.

Fry burgers in moderate amount of oil, making patties thick and about 2" in diameter. Fry at a moderate heat. Place patties in a casserole dish. Cover with water and 3 tablespoons soy sauce. Bake at 350° until most of the water is absorbed.

MONASTERY LENTILS

1 cup lentils, dry
3 cups water
1 bay leaf
1 large onion, chopped
1 carrot, chopped or grated
2 cloves garlic, minced
1/4 cup olive oil
1 cup tomatoes
1 teaspoon basil
2 tablespoons fresh parsley
2 teaspoons salt

Bring to a boil the lentils, water and bay leaf. Cover and simmer 15 minutes.

Cook onion, carrot and garlic in olive oil until soft, 3-5 minutes. Add tomatoes, and seasonings. Mix all with lentils and simmer covered for about 20 minutes or until lentils are tender. Serves 4.

SOYNUT CASSEROLE

1 cup soynuts
1 cup croutons
1/2 cup green onions, chopped
1/2 cup mushrooms
1/2 cup celery, chopped
1 can cream of mushroom soup
  diluted with 1/2 can of water or milk

Mix all ingredients. Top with another cup of croutons. Bake 30 minutes at 350°.

PECAN NUT ROAST

1/2 teaspoon Savorex
1/2 cup hot water
1½   cups bread crumbs, soft
1   tablespoon margarine
1   tablespoon flour
1/2 cup evaporated milk
1   tablespoon onion, grated
1   egg, beaten
3/4 cup pecans, chopped
1   cup mushrooms, chopped
1/2 teaspoon salt
1/2 teaspoon sage
1/2 teaspoon thyme

Dissolve Savorex in hot water. Pour over bread crumbs and toss lightly. Blend flour and margarine in saucepan over low heat. Add milk and stir until thick. Blend all ingredients together. Baked in oiled (or wax-papered) loaf pan. Bake for 20-30 minutes at 350°. Serves 8.

ZUCCHINI GARBANZO CASSEROLE

2 tablespoons oil
1 onion, chopped
1 small green pepper, diced
2 zucchini or summer squash, sliced
1 teaspoon salt
1 cup tomatoes, chopped
1/2 teaspoon oregano
1/2 teaspoon basil
1 tablespoon parsley
2 cups garbanzos, cooked

Sauté in oil the onion, pepper, zucchini and salt. Add all other ingredients and simmer 15 minutes. Or bake at 350° for 30-40 minutes. Serve as is or sprinkle with cheese. Serves 4-6.

CRUSTY CROQUETTE

1 cup white sauce, thick
2 teaspoons onion, grated
1/2 teaspoon salt
2 cups chicken style, ground
1 egg, beaten
1 cup potato chips, crushed

Combine all ingredients except egg and chips. Chill. Shape into croquette or patties. Roll in egg then chips. Repeat. Fry in deep fat - 370° until browned.

CHICKEN TOMATO POLYNESIAN

1   can (13 oz) Fri Chik soyameat*
3   medium tomatoes
2   tablespoons flour
1   teaspoon salt
2   tablespoons oil
1/2 cup onion, chopped
1   tablespoon cornstarch
1   garlic clove, minced
1   can pineapple chunks (8 ¼ ounce can)
3/4 cup broth from soyameat
    (add water to make 3/4 cup if necessary)
1   cup celery, sliced
1/2 teaspoon ginger, ground
2   tablespoons brown sugar

Cut Fri Chik in half or smaller. Cut tomatoes into wedges and set aside. Dredge chicken with a mixture of flour, salt; shake off excess. In large skillet, heat oil. Add soyameat pieces; brown about three minutes on each side. Remove and set aside. Add onion and garlic to same skillet and sauté for 2 minutes. Drain pineapple chunks, reserving one tablespoon syrup. Add pineapple to skillet along with broth, celery, sugar, ginger, and chicken. Bring to boiling point. Reduce heat and simmer covered for 15 minutes. Add reserved tomatoes, spooning some of sauce over tomatoes. Cover and simmer for five minutes. Remove chicken and tomatoes to heated platter. Blend cornstarch with reserved one tablespoon pineapple syrup. Blend into liquid in skillet, cook and stir till thickened. Spoon over soyameat and tomatoes. If desired - serve over rice.

*Worthington product, chicken style.

TUNO PATTIES

1½ tablespoons margarine
1   cup onion, chopped
3/4 cup celery, chopped
2   12-ounce rolls Tuno, frozen*
3   eggs, slightly beaten
1/2 cup mayonnaise
1   tablespoon parsley flakes
1/2 teaspoon salt
1/4 teaspoon garlic powder
1   cup bread crumbs, fine dry
3/4 cup instant mashed potato flakes

Melt margarine in skillet. Add onion and celery. Sauté at medium heat until vegetables are tender but not browned. In a large bowl combine sautéed vegetables, Tuno with liquid, eggs, mayonnaise, parsley flakes, salt and garlic powder. Blend thoroughly. Gently stir in bread crumbs and potato flakes until thoroughly blended. For each patty, place 1/4 cup Tuno mixture in a heated skillet containing about 1/8 inch vegetable oil. Flatten mixture with a spatula to about 1/2 inch thickness or more. (Patties which are too thin and large in diameter are difficult to handle while turning). Fry at medium heat until nicely browned on each side.

*Worthington Foods product Tuno frozen roll.

CASHEW CROQUETTE

2 tablespoons dehydrated onions
1/2 cup brown rice, dry
1½ cups water
1 teaspoon salt
2 cups cashews, raw
3/4 cup mushrooms, chopped
1/2 cup celery, raw and chopped
1/4 cup flour
3 tablespoons cracker meal
2 eggs
2 tablespoons parsley flakes
3/4 teaspoon MSG
1/2 teaspoon salt
2 teaspoons chicken-like seasoning
1/2 teaspoon Lawry's Seasoned Salt

Breading mixture:

3/4 cup corn flakes crumbs
1/8 teaspoon poultry seasoning
1/8 teaspoon salt
1/8 teaspoon MSG

Cover rice and onions with salted water and cook until tender (approximately 45 minutes). Grind cashews using coarse grind. Add cashews, mushrooms, celery, flour, cracker meal, eggs, parsley flakes and seasonings and mix well. Chill at least two hours. Shape into croquettes and roll in breading mixture. Croquette may be deep fat fried 1-1/2 minute at 375° and baked uncovered for 20 minutes at 350° OR baked without frying uncovered for 30 minutes at 350°. Serve with tartar sauce.

RICE AND CURRY

3   eggs
1   19-ounce can vegetarian burger
2   medium onions, chopped
2   10¾-ounce cans mushroom soup
1   13-ounce can evaporated milk
2-3 teaspoons curry powder (to taste)

Scramble eggs until well browned in small pieces. Set aside.

Sauté onions in large skillet and add vegetarian burger. Fry. Add rest of ingredients, adding the browned scrambled egg pieces last. Simmer for about 20 minutes. Serve over cooked brown rice. This is a very easy and delicious curry recipe.

Nellie Vandeman

GARBANZO LOAF

2   cups garbanzos, cooked and mashed
1   small onion, minced
4   tablespoons oil
1/2 cup nuts, chopped
1/4 cup bread crumbs
1   cup oatmeal, dry
1   cup evaporated milk
1/4 teaspoon oregano
1/2 teaspoon salt
2   eggs

Sauté onions in oil. Mix all ingredients. Pour into oiled loaf pan. Bake at 350° for 45 minutes. Unmold on a platter. Garnish. Serve with sauce (tomato, mushroom, brown or white gravy).

44

DRUMSTICKS

1   cup bread crumbs
1/2 cup mild cheese, grated
1/2 cup walnuts, chopped
1   onion, finely chopped
1   clove garlic
3   eggs and 4 egg whites
1   envelope G. Washington seasoning
salt to taste

Mix ingredients well. Form 12-15 drumsticks around sticks. Roll in corn flakes or bread crumbs. Deep fry for a few minutes to brown.

To serve: Bake at 350° for 30 minutes. Serve plain or in a mushroom soup sauce.

OATMEAL COOKIES

2   cups rolled oats
3/4 cup brown sugar
2   teaspoons orange rind, grated
1/2 teaspoon salt
1/2 cup pecans or walnuts, chopped
1/2 cup corn oil
1   egg

Combine oats, sugar, orange rind and salt. Mix well. Stir in oil. Cover and let stand few hours or overnight to blend orange flavor. Beat egg until thick and add to oatmeal mixture. Add chopped nuts. Place rounded teaspoon of mixture on ungreased baking sheet one inch apart. Bake at 350° for 12-15 minutes or until lightly browned. Do not overbake.

Nellie Vandeman

GRANOLA

5	cups rolled oats
1	cup sesame seeds
1	cup wheat germ
1	cup sunflower seeds
1	cup soy flour or whole wheat flour
1	cup coconut
1	cup raw cashew nut pieces
1	cup pecan pieces OR
	1 cup slivered almonds
2	tablespoons corn oil
2	tablespoons brown sugar
1	teaspoon vanilla
1/2	cup water

Mix all dry ingredients in large mixing bowl. In smaller bowl mix the water, oil, brown sugar and vanilla and pour over dry ingredients, stirring until blended in. Put into two shallow baking pans.

Preheat oven to 300°. Bake for 1 hour stirring every 15 minutes for first half hour and every 10 minutes for the second half hour. Turn oven down to 275° for the second half hour and watch carefully so the granola does not overbrown or burn. Let cool thoroughly. Store in airtight container. Keeps well.

Granola is delicious served over fruit, yogurt, or any hot cereal, as well as just as a cereal by itself.

Nellie Vandeman